The Fabian Society

The Fabian Society has played a central role for more than a century in the development of political ideas and public policy on the left of centre. Analysing the key challenges facing the UK and the rest of the industrialised world in a changing society and global economy, the Society's programme aims to explore the political ideas and the policy reforms which will define progressive politics in the new century.

The Society is unique among think tanks in being a democratically-constituted membership organisation. It is affiliated to the Labour Party but is editorially and organisationally independent. Through its publications, seminars and conferences, the Society provides an arena for open-minded public debate.

Fabian Society
11 Dartmouth Street
London SW1H 9BN
www.fabian-society.org.uk

Fabian ideas
Series editor: Ellie Levenson

First published December 2002

ISBN 0 7163 0604 2
ISSN 1469 0136

British Library Cataloguing in Publication data.
A catalogue record for this book is available from the British Library.

Contents

Introduction   1

1 | Food in schools   5

2 | Advertising to children   10

3 | Educating parents   14

4 | Food poverty   17

5 | Children and exercise   23

6 | Conclusion   31

References   35

About the authors

Dr Howard Stoate has been the Member of Parliament for Dartford since 1997. He is the Chair of the All Party Parliamentary Group on Primary Care and Public Health, Co-chair of the All-Party Parliamentary Group on Obesity and Secretary of the Parliamentary Labour Party Health Committee. He is also a practising GP and a Fellow of Royal College of General Practitioners.

Bryan Jones is Researcher to Dr Howard Stoate.

Introduction

Our assumption that barring a major economic meltdown of the kind that happened in Russia after the fall of the Soviet Union, life expectancy in the UK will continue to rise indefinitely is looking ever more tenuous. Seriously obese children are losing up to nine years on average through diseases that were not as common among their parents warns Andrew Prentice, professor of international hygiene at the London School of Hygiene and Tropical Medicine who believes that a paradigm shift is taking place in public health in Britain.[1]

He believes that the now epidemic levels of childhood obesity in the UK will result in thousands of children pre-deceasing their parents. The number of obese children in the UK has doubled in the last ten years and around 10 per cent of children are now officially obese and at serious risk of developing any number of potentially life threatening conditions such as diabetes, heart disease and circulatory disorders.[2]

Even if Professor Prentice is proved to be wrong and we develop the drugs and treatment to ensure that an increasingly debilitated population lives ever longer, it is highly likely that our 'healthspan', that is the period of our life which is free from chronic or debilitating illness, will get shorter.

Not only is obesity bad news for children, it is bad news for the

Treasury and even worse news for the economy. In 1998, the cost to the NHS of treating obesity related conditions was already close to £500 million. The loss to the economy through 18 million days of sickness and 40 million working days lost through premature death, was nearly £2 billion.[3]

The picture looks even bleaker when you look at some of the statistics relating to diabetes. One study put the annual cost of treating diabetes at nearly £5.2 billion.[4] That is 9 per cent of the NHS Budget in 2000, and that is only taking into account the people with diabetes that we know about. Diabetes UK estimates that there are a million people with the condition who have yet to be diagnosed, let alone receive treatment. More worrying still is that the first teenagers are now being diagnosed with Type 2 diabetes, a condition which is closely linked with obesity and is usually only found in those aged over 40.

Type 2 diabetes is a chronic, multi-system disease. The likelihood of a patient developing major complications is directly proportional to the length of time he or she has the disease. If you develop it at the age of 75 you are quite likely to die of something else first. However, anyone getting it in their teens runs a high risk of visual impairment, leg amputations, renal failure requiring dialysis or transplantation, or premature death from heart disease. Quite apart from the human cost and suffering, the cost to the NHS of treating the complications of large numbers of diabetics will be staggering. In fact it makes Sir Derek Wanless' striking recent estimate that effective public health measures put in place now could save the NHS around £30 billion, or 20 per cent of its budget, by 2022 look slightly conservative.

None of this news can come as much of a surprise. In the last few years the public has been bombarded by scare stories warning of the health time bomb that lies in wait for our offspring. No one believes any more that childhood obesity is just a cosmetic problem.

Not enough is being done to educate young people about food and nutrition or to challenge the sedentary culture that prevails in so many households in this country.

The habits that children learn in their first few years stay with them for the rest of their lives. If we can get our children into the habit of eating a varied and balanced diet and exercising regularly by the time they leave primary school, then we will have gone a long way towards ensuring that as they get older they will not be faced with the same array of chronic health problems as their parents and grandparents.

In this pamphlet we shall be putting forward a series of measures designed to encourage young people to eat better, exercise frequently and take more responsibility for their health. As well as food education in schools and the role of sport we shall also be considering the impact of food advertising on children and taking a look at food labelling.

We also look at food poverty in Britain. The connection between food poverty during childhood and low health outcomes is well established. Children that are born with a low birth weight and are nutritionally deprived in early infancy and in childhood are at a higher than average risk of developing heart disease or a chronic disease later in life and dying young.

A boy born today in Manchester for example, where 27 of the city's 33 wards are among the 10 per cent most deprived in the country, is very unlikely to see his 70th birthday. A boy born at the same time to a family in Dorset however, can look forward to living ten years longer than his Manchester equivalent.[5]

It is a horrifying statistic. It means that large swathes of our population stand to lose up to a decade off their lives simply because they are born in the wrong place and into the wrong class. Even if those children go on to do well in life and as adults eat all the right things and exercise regularly, they may not be able to undo the damage done to their long-term health prospects during those first few years of life.

Finally we will examine the state of public health in the modern NHS. We will argue that too much emphasis is still being placed on acute sector medicine and that as a consequence patients are becoming too reliant on high tech medical solutions to their problems. In this climate it is extremely difficult to encourage children and young adults to take responsibility for their own health or recognise the importance of disease prevention. We will be exploring ways in which we can reverse this trend and put disease prevention at centre of NHS work.

1 | Food in schools

In an ideal world it would be left to parents to teach their children about food and nutrition. It is becoming increasingly apparent though that many parents are as ignorant about food as their children. In a recent study carried out by Mintel, 70 per cent of the parents with young children interviewed admitted that they do not know enough about food and nutrition to feed their children healthily.[6]

The onus is therefore very much on schools to inform children about healthy eating and the Government has recognised this. A National Healthy Schools Programme, a joint initiative between the Department of Health and the Department for Education and Skills has now been set up. One of the programme's principal aims is to encourage healthy eating in schools. Schools are being asked to provide, promote and monitor healthier food at lunch and break times and at breakfast clubs.

Though current legislation in England makes it clear that the presentation and content of school meals is a matter for local authorities and schools alone to decide upon, the Government has also set out for the first time compulsory minimum nutritional standards for school meals. Providing that proper monitoring takes place, this will ensure that all schools observe at least some basic nutritional criteria in preparing their menus. As the school lunch is still the main meal of the day for many children this is especially important.

In addition, the new National School Fruit Scheme has enabled over 80,000 four to six year olds in over 500 schools in the Government's Health Action Zones to receive a free piece of fruit every day. As many of these children have limited diets and rarely get the chance to eat fresh fruit or vegetables, this scheme has an obvious nutritional payoff. Not only this, the scheme has succeeded in widening the food horizons of thousands of children at a critical point in their lives. It may not stop them from making burgers, crisps and chocolate their food of choice, but hopefully it will ensure that they continue to eat fruit as well.

If children are exposed to food like this from a young enough age, then provided of course that their experience is a positive one, they are less likely to be turned off by it as they get older. As Professor Jane Wardle, co-founder of the charity Weight Concern has pointed out, many children are by instinct ill disposed to any sort of food that comes with a healthy living tag.[7] In their minds, healthy food means dull, tasteless food. However, if they have always eaten it and always liked it, then the chances are that they will see it as a nice food that just happens to be healthy as well.

In the same way, banning crisps, chocolate and fizzy drinks from school canteens and vending machines as some schools have done, having decided that they are not the sorts of foods that children should be eating, might also be counterproductive. It is good to see schools taking the diet of their pupils seriously enough that they are prepared to lose valuable income from vending machine sales, but as we know prohibiting something usually only has the effect of making it seem more attractive.

There is nothing wrong with schools serving up burgers and chips to their pupils at lunchtime provided that they are served only occasionally and there are other fruit and vegetable options available. Likewise, selling fizzy drinks in school is justifiable as long as there are plenty of healthier alternatives on offer and their availability is very strictly limited.

If on the other hand children are spending their money on fizzy drinks because they do not fancy drinking from an unhygienic looking water fountain in the toilets and are still thirsty after their one beaker of warm water in the canteen at lunchtime, then we need to think again.

Unfortunately drinking water facilities are limited or non-existent in many schools. In 50 per cent of schools drinking water fountains in the toilets are the only source of fresh water and in nearly 10 per cent of schools there are no facilities at all.[8]

British schools have always been lukewarm about the idea of children having drinking facilities in the classroom. Access to fresh water in the workplace has remained a privilege available only to adults. In those countries where such an indulgence is permitted, order and discipline in the classroom has not collapsed and children have been able to learn the importance of re-hydrating themselves regularly.

If we are to wean children off their dependence on sugar rich fizzy drinks and get in the habit of drinking water more regularly then surely we need to adopt a similar policy in this country. In terms of the long term benefits to the health of children, the cost of putting a water cooler in each classroom is a policy that would more than pay for itself.

However, the policy change that we most need is for food education to be included in the curriculum. The best way for children to learn about food is for them to touch it, smell it and above all taste it. We can change school dinner menus as much as we like, but unless children are given a grounding in cooking and have some understanding about what it is they are eating and the effect it will have on them, they will not have the skills or knowledge to carry on eating properly when they leave school.

Unfortunately schools have found it difficult in recent years to find room in the curriculum for food education due to the increasingly heavy demands placed on it by core curriculum subjects. A lack of specialist equipment and facilities in schools and also a shortage of properly qualified staff have also been a factor. There is a statutory obligation for primary schools to offer food technology lessons (the subject which has replaced home economics) but no such obligation exists at secondary level. The Government strongly recommends that schools offer students the opportunity to study food technology, but around 10 per cent of schools offer nothing at all and many more only have the resources to give their students a cursory introduction to the subject.

Even more of a concern is the fact that only a small part of the food technology syllabus actually covers cooking and nutrition. In secondary schools for example much of the responsibility for teaching the students about nutrition and healthy eating is left to science teachers and those giving personal and social education lessons. As these teachers are not food specialists and cannot give their students the benefit of any hands-on teaching, one suspects that most of these lessons do little to inspire or enlighten children. Even children studying food technology spend very little time with food in front of them. They are much more likely to spend a lesson designing and creating the packaging for some biscuits than they are to have a lesson in which they actually make some biscuits as food technology tends to be run by design and technology departments as opposed to people whose first and foremost interest is food. Indeed an understanding of design and production methods is seen almost as more important in a food technology teacher nowadays than the ability to cook.

It would be no more than a pyrrhic victory then if food education was included in the secondary curriculum, but all we ended up with was the same Food Technology syllabus. To make a meaningful difference we need a food education syllabus that is focused on food and gives children the chance to get their hands dirty and discover what food is really all about. Cooking by its very nature does not deliver measurable outcomes that can be assessed and moderated like other more academic subjects, but that should not mean it should be excluded from the curriculum.

It would mean investing in kitchens and equipment in schools and it would mean changing the way teachers in this area are trained. Schools would also have to have extra money to buy the food and materials for pupils to use in lessons otherwise children from the poorest families would not be able to take part in them.

It would be money well spent. Making food education a key part of the syllabus and putting in the requisite investment will help to drive home the message to children that healthy eating is a serious issue and not something to be taken lightly.

2 | Advertising to children

At present British advertising guidelines forbid the advertising of alcohol or potentially dangerous products to children. They also specify that adverts should not give children a misleading impression of the scale or capability of a product. These guidelines are easy to enforce and are not in any way controversial. Where it becomes more difficult for the regulators to step in is in cases where an advert gives a jaundiced, but not in itself misleading, impression of a product by failing to disclose the possible risks in using it.

Adverts for food products high in saturated fats, sugar or salt, do not of course reveal that regular consumption of them has a detrimental effect on our health or make the point that they should be eaten as part of a balanced diet. Moreover, because they appear on our screens so frequently, and are not counterbalanced by adverts for any unprocessed food products, they project a totally unbalanced nutritional message that is wholly at odds with Government guidelines on healthy eating.

Sustain, an organisation that campaigns for better food and farming, estimates that between 95 per cent and 99 per cent of adverts for food appearing during television programmes for children are for products that are high in fat, sugar and salt.[9] They also point out that there are twice as many adverts for products like this during Saturday morning television than there are after the post nine o'clock watershed. Nor is there anything to stop companies from sponsoring programmes aimed at children should they so wish. Broadcasting rules prevent them from displaying their products on screen, but they are entitled to put their logo on the screen whenever there is an advertising break. The fast food chain McDonalds came in for heavy criticism from food campaigners earlier this year when it signed a £1m deal to sponsor GMTV's early morning weekend show, Diggit, specifically aimed at children.

The company has also been criticised, along with Burger King and a host of other crisps and confectionary manufacturers, for promoting a range of products linked to the World Cup. Food charities including the Food Commission complained that celebrity endorsements of these products by top footballers, supposedly the paragons of healthy living, would cause lasting damage to the campaign to encourage healthier patterns of eating amongst children.[10]

Some countries have reacted to this selective targeting of children by fast food chains and the food and drinks industry by introducing codes of conduct for advertisers or, in the case of Sweden, banning all advertising aimed at the under twelves. The Swedes, who have some of the best health outcomes in Europe, have argued that without a complete ban across the board, it is hard to stop companies targeting children and seeking to establish brand preferences amongst them.

With the Government now pursuing legislation to ban tobacco advertising outright, why should we not go one-step further and ban food and drink advertising to children? After all more people are now falling ill because of obesity than because of smoking.[11] A ban would give schools and health education bodies a genuine opportunity to disseminate the healthy eating message to children and to help change the way they eat.

Confectionary and snack manufacturers and fast food companies have a right to advertise their product, but we have reached the stage now where adverts for their products are dominating our airwaves and our print media to the exclusion of all else. The one-sided nutritional message that children are getting as a result certainly is not good for their health. Nor is it good for the long-term health of the food and drinks industry. Fear over the consequences of obesity is growing in this country. With the public and the press looking for someone to blame, the industry could easily find itself demonised in the same way that the cigarette manufacturers are. Far from restricting consumer freedoms such a ban would enable young people to make a more informed choice as adult consumers about the food they eat, having had the opportunity to learn about food as children in an environment free from undue external influences.

No doubt some will also try and portray such a ban as simply another move by an increasingly puritanical food lobby to undermine a legitimate business. But this ban would not be about penalizing the food industry though. Sweet and snack manufacturers have been a part of British manufacturing for hundreds of years and will continue to be so for many years ahead. They are an industry that fulfils a need. The purpose of this ban would not be to prevent children from eating chocolate and crisps and so on but to help them to be more discriminating as to when and in what quantity they eat them. We want children to see products like these as the occasional luxuries they once were as opposed to the staple foods that they are threatening to become. I would also suggest that the Government ensures that commercial sponsorship schemes involving schools and events in which schoolchildren participate, especially those by food and drink manufacturers, are properly policed and regulated.

Private sector sponsorship of school activities is to be encouraged where it will lead to children taking part in activities that otherwise they would not be able to, but it has to be carefully managed. Schools need to be alert to the motives of the companies that approach them. Otherwise they can easily become the unwitting stooges of companies looking for a bit of instant credibility in the community or businesses whose sole interest is to boost their sales figures.

Accepting a sportswear company's offer of a free day of specialist sports coaching for example, is reasonable enough, providing that it is not being used by the company as an opportunity to promote a specific product or line. Allowing a confectionary manufacturer to sponsor a healthy eating programme or sports competition is clearly unacceptable.

Also of concern are the marketing campaigns of certain snack manufacturers encouraging parents and children to buy their product in order to raise funds for new books and equipment in their school. This kind of strategy undermines the efforts of schools to encourage children to follow a balanced diet and should be explicitly condemned by the Department for Education and Skills.

Perhaps what we require in order to protect schools is a code of practice for the private sector to which all companies that give money, time or resources to schools are legally obliged to sign up. There should also be specific guidance material for schools entering sponsorship deals and officers available to advise schools directly about individual deals.

This framework is important if lines of good practice are to emerge and we are to avoid going down the same line as the United States where food and drink manufacturers can make significant contributions to school budgets in return for exposure in the school and brand loyalty from students.

3 | Educating parents

To help parents become more discerning in the food they buy for their children, companies have to be more honest in the way they label their products. The Food Standards Agency is making laudable efforts on behalf of the consumer to tighten up on labelling and to ensure that the nutritional information on packaging is presented in a user friendly form free from ambiguities and sophistries, but more needs to be done.

According to the Food and Drink Federation, over 80 per cent of manufactured products in the UK carry nutrition labelling, yet there is considerable doubt as to whether consumers understand or even read these labels. One recent survey carried out by Safeway revealed that only one in five people know what RDA (Recommended Daily Allowance) stands for.[18]

Consumers have also complained about the sheer number of different healthy eating messages that appear on labels and have said that they find it difficult to gauge the value or relative importance of each of them. Messages such as 'low fat' and 'low in saturated fat' leave consumers confused and no better informed. Another frequent complaint is that some products give nutritional values per 100g or per serving whereas other products just give them by the contents.

Consumers want to see manufacturers employ simpler, standardised and, above all, spin free language on their packaging. Instead of labels saying that they are low fat or a certain per cent fat free, they want to be told how much fat is in the product they are buying.

The Government should draw up a universal nutritional code incorporating a handful of readily recognisable symbols and a set vocabulary that is as transparent as possible. The aim would be to have a nutritional code that is as familiar to consumers as the road signs in the Highway Code are to drivers.

Consumers also have a right to reliable independent information giving them clear guidance about how much fat and what sort of fat they and their children should be eating.

There is already a lot of information out there. In every supermarket in Britain consumers can pick up an impressive range of advice leaflets and suggested menus and there is no shortage of information on the internet and in the press. But what we do not have is a universally recognised and trusted source of dietary advice and information. Not since the British Standard Diet was published during the Second World War to support the introduction of rationing, has the public had access to a definitive guide to precisely what and how much we should be eating, day by day, week by week.

It is unlikely that anything as overtly prescriptive as the British Standard Diet will be published again, at least not in this country. It would be impossible to arrive at a diet that even remotely satisfied the heterogeneous nutritional, social and cultural requirements of the British population, and there would be justifiable uproar if any Government attempted it.

Nevertheless, it ought to be possible for the Department of Health to come up with a set of broad nutritional guidelines incorporating advice about recommended daily amounts for the average man, woman or child, what foods contain and even some suggested daily menus.

Some nutritional guidelines have been posted on the NHS Direct website, though they are short on relevant figures and difficult to locate. There is nothing on the subject in Department of Health's online health advice leaflets.

The United States Government regularly publishes a brochure called *Dietary Guidance for Americans* that gives recommended daily calorific intakes and nutritional information about specific foods without incurring the wrath of either the food industry, lobby groups or Wall Street. Surely the same could be done here.

If the Government took the decision to send an officially sanctioned National Nutritional Guide to every home and school in Britain it would transform the profile of public health in this country at a stroke. It would help to explode the myth that the health of the nation begins and ends at the hospital gate or in the GP's waiting room and would allow us to hammer home the importance of healthy eating. As well as giving families the armoury of information they need to eat healthily, it would also help to sweep away much of the misinformation, ignorance and confusion that surrounds diet and nutrition in Britain.

A grand gesture like this might prove to be the catalyst the healthy eating campaign so desperately needs. Winning the hearts and minds of the people is one of the biggest challenges we face.

4| Food poverty

In Britain hundreds of people die every week as a direct result of poor nutrition. Not all of these people come from low income families but there is no doubt that poverty places people at a higher than average risk of dying prematurely and getting ill.

The richest 10 per cent of families spend more than £100 a week on food, the poorest 10 per cent spend just £25 a week and frequently go without essential food items in order to pay other more pressing household bills, according to the Child Poverty Action Group.[13]

Low incomes and the easy availability of credit have had the effect of locking a large number of families into a cycle of debt and poverty, making healthy food an expendable luxury.

The Government has done a great deal to raise the incomes of low income families. The introduction of the Working Families Tax Credit, the Minimum Income Guarantee for pensioners, a national minimum wage and income support for single parents have seen the incomes of the poorest 10 per cent rise by 13 per cent since 1997. There is no doubt though that further increases are necessary if the long-term health prospects of the very poorest families are to improve.

According to a Joseph Rowntree foundation report published

two years ago, around four million people in Britain cannot afford to eat healthily.[14] Other studies have shown that one in four pregnant women find it difficult to afford a healthy diet.[15]

For many poorer families the problem is compounded by the fact that their access to good, cheap, fresh food is severely limited. The major food retailers in Britain cater for the car owning majority, not for those families who cannot afford to buy or run a car. With most new supermarkets situated on the edge of towns, well away from council estates and other areas of high density housing, many families are forced to rely on local convenience stores closer to home.

Not only are these local independent stores expensive, but they also offer very little in the way of fresh produce. What little they do stock is often far less fresh than that on offer in the supermarkets. Faced by a choice between a processed oven ready product, which may be high in saturated fat, salt, sugar and carbohydrates but will at least fill you up, and some expensive vegetables that are past their best, it is hardly surprising that many low income families are nutritionally deprived.

Thousands of families though do not even have this option. In the last decade 60,000 small shops have disappeared.[16] Unsurprisingly the exodus has been the most marked in the poorer urban areas and small rural villages.

Independent stores cannot compete with the food retailing giants who in recent years have relentlessly squeezed the profit margins on their food lines in order to get customers into their stores. The supermarkets are now using profits on their non-food lines to subsidise cuts in their food prices in the same way as the petrol retailers compete on the price of a gallon of petrol in order to get more customers into their profit-making shops.

For example, in the two most deprived wards in my constituency of Dartford, both of which have been hit hard by the closure of local shops in recent years, non car owning residents are now a ten minute bus or train ride away from the nearest major supermarket.

The story is the same across the country. In Govan, a deprived area of Glasgow where the life expectancy of a child is ten years lower than in the most affluent parts of Glasgow, most local shops have now closed their doors. There is a new hypermarket on the edge of Govan which is easy to get to by car, but virtually impossible to get to by foot.

A recent survey by the Rural Development Commission of parishes with less than 10,000 showed over two thirds of them now have no general store.[17] One way of addressing this problem is to encourage the food retail giants to set up stores closer to where people live.

Some of the supermarket chains have retained a presence in town centres by re-launching 'Express' or 'Metro' stores, but few are keen to open stores in the council built estates where the need for new outlets is greatest. Most Chief Executives say that these estates, mostly designed in the twenty or thirty years after the war, simply are not built to support modern supermarkets. They also complain about the restrictive nature of current planning regulations. However, there have been some success stories. In Hulme in Manchester, a large council built estate was pulled down and replaced by a new housing development incorporating a successful supermarket that is equally accessible to car owning and non-car owning residents.

We should also look to the planning process to help us deliver the kind of universally accessible, community centred supermarkets that we want. New stores should only get approval if the applicants can demonstrate to the planning authority that a minimum number of people, set out in the local plan, can get to the store by foot within quarter of an hour. The applicants should also have to include in their proposal a series of dedicated pedestrian access routes. Radical measures like this may ultimately prove to be the most effective solution in large-scale urban estates where has always been difficult to maintain a meaningful retail and leisure element.

In tandem with this approach we need a strategy that will encourage more locally run neighbourhood shops and amenities selling cheap fresh produce to local people to open up. This is important not just from a nutritional perspective, but also in terms of helping communities to regain their self-respect and sense of identity.

The kind of communities designated as food poor, such as inner city estates, rural parishes and mining villages, have been hit hard psychologically by closure of local services and traditional employers. This loss of purpose has caused lasting damage to these communities and has had a measurable impact on the health prospects of the people living in them.

In a number of communities this decline has been partially offset by the development of community food projects run by local people. The primary goal of these projects has been to improve access to fresh food by giving people the chance to buy cheap produce from local food co-ops or by setting up cafes serving healthy meals at affordable prices. Some projects have also attempted to improve cooking skills and understanding of food and nutrition by encouraging people to 'cook and eat' sessions and other workshops.

Aside from the obvious nutritional benefits these schemes have yielded, food projects have also helped to boost the confidence and sense of self-worth of those involved in them. In many cases they have had an energising effect on the community and have helped to strengthen the ties holding it together.

But food projects represent only a partial solution. Their success is often founded on the dynamism and energy of few highly motivated individuals and they can quickly run into problems if these people leave or funding problems emerge, however well entrenched in the community they seem to be. Ensuring their long-term, sustainable success is not easy. Because their success is so contingent on local circumstances and local personalities it would be virtually impossible to set up a comprehensive network of food projects across the country. Provision would inevitably be patchy.

We should also question whether food projects are what people want. They may fulfil immediate needs but in terms of tackling the growing gulf between the lifestyles and expectations of the majority of the population and those at the bottom end of society, they are of little help. They may even help to reinforce the divide. Many people find it demeaning to have to rely on services which are specifically geared towards low income families. They want access to the same range of local shops and services as the majority of the population.

However, we are not going to get a renaissance of the small independent retailer unless we have some fairly sizeable incentives on offer. One possibility is to offer a tax credit to retailers who are prepared to set up shop in areas designated as food poor. To qualify a shop would have devote a significant percentage of their floor space to fresh produce and stick within an agreed price threshold. Provided that the owner was still able to make a reasonable profit from the business and the tax credit was available each year, not just as a one-off benefit, there is no reason why it should not be widely taken up.

Alternatively we could offer a tax credit to established businesses who were willing to allow budding local entrepreneurs to set up a small low rent concession or stall on their premises. This would allow local people with little experience of running a business and limited capital to establish a foothold in the market and to hone their business skills.

It is an approach that could re-invigorate our high streets and create hundreds of local jobs as well as transforming the eating habits of thousands of our poorest families. It would demonstrate to retailers and developers across the country that you can sell quality products in poorer areas and that pound shops and fast food outlets are not the only shops that can survive in this sort of environment.

5| Children and exercise

t is not easy staying fit if you are a child in twenty-first century Britain. There are so many distractions and diversions on offer to today's children, that they scarcely have time to get bored, let alone fit. Competition for attention is fierce and with millions being poured into developing ever more sophisticated and spectacular gaming concepts, it is hardly surprising that traditional pastimes such as football, bat and ball and hide and seek have lost their appeal. Who needs a playground when you've got a PlayStation?[18] Children are now so chair-bound that according to the British Heart Foundation, a third of children between the ages of two and seven do not even do the minimum recommended level of exercise a week.

Not only do over a third of parents not know how much exercise their children should be taking, but because of their own sedentary lifestyles they are failing to set the right example for their children. The chances are that if the parents spend most of their free time in front of the television, then their children will too.[10]

Some parents also prefer to keep their children indoors where they can keep an eye on them. A survey by the Children's Society showed that 15 per cent of parents refuse to let their children play outdoors because they are worried about the possibility of them being approached by strangers.[20] The same survey also revealed that children themselves are deterred from playing outside because of the fear factor. Nearly a fifth of children are worried by the dangers posed by traffic and a quarter of them are worried about being bullied by older children.

Peer culture is also having an effect. The vast majority of girls choose to opt out of PE at school as soon as they possibly can, and very few of them are still playing any form of organised sport by the time they reach their mid teens. Their distaste for sport, or indeed any exercise, is such that by the age of fifteen, two thirds of girls fall into the physically inactive category.[21]

This declining level of activity combined with escalating calorific intakes is, as we know, having a devastating effect on the health of British children. The prospects for improvement are not great. We know that giving children an exercise habit when they are young is vital if they are going to carry on taking exercise when they are adults, but measures to ensure this happens are thin on the ground.

We have a wealth of green spaces in our towns and cities and over one hundred thousand voluntary sport and leisure clubs across the country, the vast majority of which have the ability to cater for children, yet we make little use of either resource. Traffic, fear of crime or intimidation, dirty and poorly maintained facilities and a lack of time have led to a decline in use of public parks and playgrounds by children.

To make these amenities more appealing to parents and children, we need first all to invest in the equipment and facilities there to make sure they are safe to use and as attractive and child-friendly as possible. We also have to make it easier for children and parents to walk or cycle to such amenities from home. This means creating safer road crossings, dedicated cycle lanes and, where necessary, better lighting. Wherever possible pedestrians and cyclists should be given priority by road planners, especially in heavily built up areas. We need more 'home zones'and 'Quiet Lanes'.

We also need to address the fear of crime. The public have made it clear time and again that they want to see a greater uniformed presence on our streets and in public places, whether police officers or park or street wardens. The gradual withdrawal of beat officers together with a decline in the number of auxiliary agents of authority in the community such as park wardens and caretakers, have convinced the public that the authorities are not interested in tackling the everyday problems which beset their lives such as vandalism, graffiti and yobbish behaviour by bored adolescents. Visible patrols may not in themselves add much to the crime fighting capability of the police and our other law enforcement agencies, but they have the effect of reassuring anxious parents, who believe that we have ceded control of the streets to street robbers and vandals.

It is not an irrational belief. The 'broken windows' theory of James Wilson and George Kelling suggests that criminal activity and anti-social behaviour tends to be concentrated in the areas where the hand of law and order is the least conspicuous[31]. Usually these tend to be the most down at heel areas but this is not always the case. It is interesting to note that street crime rose sharply in the prosperous outer London boroughs in the after-math of the 11th September 2001 attacks on New York, when hundreds of police officers were transferred from their duties in outer London to Central London, creating a vacuum of authority.

The new Police Reform Act allows for the appointment of community support officers for the first time and gives us the opportunity to provide the extra uniformed presence in the community that the public want. Their brief will be to tackle precisely the kind of low-level disorder and petty offences that the public come into contact with and fear most. Provided that enough officers can be recruited, and the initial signs are good, then there is a good chance that they will help to significantly reduce the public's fear of crime.

As well as encouraging parents to let their children play outside, it would also persuade more of them to let their children walk to school on their own. At present only one in eleven primary school children travel to school unaccompanied, compared to one in five a decade ago.[22]

We also need to ensure that young people are consulted when new play spaces and amenities are being designed. There is no point investing money in facilities that are not going to be used. The needs of older children must not be ignored either. Unless we invest in the sort of facilities that they want such as skateboard parks, off road biking circuits, assault courses and their own shelters, they will either carry on congregating in playgrounds preventing young children from using them or simply stay at home.

Some Primary Care Trusts have tried to build partnerships with local clubs and associations in a bid to get more people involved in sport and exercise. This approach has had successes but if we are to get children into the habit of playing sport or exercising outside of school hours then we also need to engage the support of schools and local education authorities.

By forging links with local clubs and municipal leisure centres and encouraging them to provide coaching sessions at specific times during the week for children, schools could help to make extra-curricular sport much more accessible. It would also ensure that children get introduced to a much wider range of sports and leisure activities than the schools themselves are able to provide. This could be of particular benefit to girls, many of whom are totally turned off by the limited diet of competitive, team-based sports that they get offered at school.

The other obvious advantage this approach would have is that it would encourage youngsters to carry on visiting these clubs in the evenings and at weekends even when they have left school. At the moment a lot of young people, even those who enjoyed sport at school, stop playing sport and exercising regularly the moment they get a full-time job and no longer have sport timetabled into their schedule.

However, if leisure centres and sports clubs are going to let children use their facilities without charge, most clubs are going to require extra funds from to meet additional running costs. The Government would therefore have to make grants available to any club participating in the scheme.

Regrettably, school sport and physical education classes have suffered the same fate as food education in the last few years. Lack of space in the curriculum, lack of facilities and lack of staff have all taken their toll. The National Playing Fields Association points to a huge drop in the number school playing fields over the last few decades. Though the decline has now slowed schools are still looking to sell off parts of their playgrounds or playing fields in order to raise extra resources for new equipment or new classrooms. Many schools now have more pupils on their rolls than twenty years ago but less space in which they can play sport.

Only around a third of secondary school children receive two or more hours a week of physical education, compared to nearly half in the mid nineties. There has been an even greater decline in Primary Schools. In the last five years the amount of time spent by primary school children in physical education lessons has more or less halved.[23] The Government's White Paper, *Schools - achieving success* gave a commitment that all children will be entitled to two hours of physical education and school sport a week, within and outside the curriculum, but there is clearly a lot to do before that pledge can be realised. Money is being made available by the New Opportunities Fund, the Department of Culture, Media and Sport and the Department for

Education and Skills to enhance and refurbish existing sports facilities, particularly in deprived areas, but this is only the start.

We do not just need better equipment and facilities; we also need better teaching. Training for primary school teachers puts very little emphasis on sport and the Qualifications and Curriculum Authority does not offer teachers much in the way of guidance for teaching physical education. With teachers left very much to their own devices it is hardly surprising that many children do not find it as interesting and exciting as they might and look to opt out whenever possible.

Swan Valley Community School in Swanscombe, North Kent is a new PFI funded school. It has just opened a state of the art fitness suite, a huge success with both boys and girls at the school. It has attracted a large number of children who had hitherto shown no interest in sport whatsoever.

More schools need to think along these lines. Instead of forcing children on to the football or hockey field every winter in the wind and rain and telling them that it is for their own good, schools should spend some time listening to their pupils and finding out what it is that they actually want to do.

Many teenagers may not fancy running around a muddy field in the cold but they quite like the idea of using a treadmill for half an hour with their personal stereo on or using some weights.

Perhaps the Government could consider giving secondary schools a one-off payment to buy some exercise and fitness equipment. It would certainly show that it was in touch with the mood and aspirations of teenagers.

Another big problem that we have to address is access to school facilities. The key to sustaining interest in sport is to make sure that there is access to school facilities and equipment not just after school but at weekends and during school holidays. A child cannot be expected to develop a lasting interest in, for example, cricket, if the only chance they get to pick up a bat and ball is during a few lessons at the end of the summer term. If they like the game they find get very frustrated when they have to drop it the moment term ends. Inevitably their enthusiasm for the sport soon cools. Schools should keep their sports halls and fields open for their pupils, and their parents, all year round. What better way could there be of putting sport at the heart of the community? The Government could use some of the money now being poured into school sports to train community volunteers or recruit paid supervisors to do the job. It will not attract every child away from computer games or the television but as it is lack of opportunity rather than apathy that prevents many children from playing sport, there is no reason why it should not be a success.

I would also like to see responsibility for school sport and community sport transferred to the Department of Health. Lumping sport with culture and media in one ministry as we do at the moment serves to further reinforce the view that sport is first and foremost an entertainment form and something you watch other people play rather than play yourself. It makes it difficult to persuade the public that sport is anything other than a minority activity, suitable only for the fittest and strongest of us. We have to challenge this culture. We should split sport into two parts; the multi-million pound entertainment industry played by professionals would remain the responsibility of the Department for Culture, Media and Sport while the responsibility for community sport, played in spare time for enjoyment and keeping fit, should be transferred to the Department of Health. This would highlight the link between sport, exercise and good health. It was done in Cuba many years ago as part of a wide ranging programme of primary care reforms and the country now has health outcomes which compare favourably with those of many first world countries, despite its lack of resources. It would also help to democratise sport and give the message that although sporting excellence is important, sport as a means of allowing people to stay fit and healthy is more important. Sport is for everyone, not just the talented few, and you do not have to be of a specific age, shape or size to get involved.

6| Conclusion

When the National Helath Service was launched in 1948, the British public had good reason to celebrate. Here for the first time was a healthcare system accessible to everyone regardless of income or background. It was a triumphant moment for progressive socialism. It represented precisely the kind of democratic, egalitarian institution for which millions had first fought for and then voted for in the 1945 landslide.

Fifty years later and the social landscape in which the NHS exists is very different. The consumer revolution and the new individualism which emerged in the 1960s and 1970s and became entrenched in the 1980s has helped to weaken the relationship between the patient and the health service. We are still proud of the NHS and most of us still want to see the principles on which it was founded jealously protected, but we tend to view the NHS from the perspective of a consumer rather than a stakeholder.

In some ways the NHS has become just another service provider, a service which we pay for through taxes and national insurance contributions, and from which we expect a high quality of personal service. In this respect there is little tangible difference in the way we view the NHS to the way we view a high street optician or even a high street travel agent.

As the Prime Minister has recently pointed out, patients now want an NHS which recognises them as individuals and can offer them a service which is tailored to their personal needs.[36] 'The one size fits all' health service model is no longer viable in today's market society.

In many ways this consumerisation of the NHS is a positive development. The NHS needs smarter, savvier and more quality conscious patients if services are to improve and develop. The kind of passive and deferential patient of old who asked few questions may be good for helping trusts keep to appointment targets but they also produce complacent practitioners and a culture of intransigence.

Although service quality is improving, is the health of patients? Patients may be better equipped to press for the treatment to which they think they are entitled, but though gym memberships are on the up there are few signs other than that they are any more prepared to take responsibility for their own health than they were a generation ago.

This does not bode well for our children. As long as the burden of responsibility for keeping the nation healthy falls exclusively on the shoulders of health professionals and not to any extent on patients, then our long-term health prospects and those of our children are unlikely to improve much. The difficulty is that in our society, as in just about every advanced market economy, we perceive health as something that inevitably gets worse with age, but that can restored quickly and efficiently through the intervention of trained professionals. With thousands of doctors and nurses, equipped with the very latest medical technology, being paid to keep us healthy, why should we as clients expend any energy caring for our bodies?

It is hardly surprising therefore that we are such an unhealthy society and that our children are becoming less and less fit by the year. The NHS is making laudable efforts to arrest this decline, by promoting healthier living, prioritising disease prevention and driving home the message that our health is in our own hands, but the message is not being heard.

To some extent we are fighting a losing battle in raising the prifle of public health. It is not a major talking point on the doorstep at election time. Public health has the reputation of being a rather dry and inchoate issue, which though worthy and important does not set pulses racing. Despite this the Government has set out an array of ambitious public health targets. It has also appointed a public health minister to spearhead its strategy and to co-ordinate efforts across Government.

Even with these measures, steering attention towards disease prevention has proven to be decidedly difficult. To do this will require a fundamental change in the nature of the relationship between the NHS and the patient. What we need is a contract between the provider and the client, setting out for the first time what each party has a right to expect from each other and referring explicitly to disease prevention and what patients should be doing to stay healthy as well as explaining what the NHS should be doing for them.

The NHS clearly does not have the right to set itself up as a moral arbiter of the lifestyle choices made by the general public. However, it does have the right to make value judgements about patients' lifestyles. The NHS has a professional duty to act according to what it considers to be the medical best interests of individual patients and also the community of users as a whole. GPs do not have enough time to talk to their patients aboutgeneral disease prevention. In most consultations they only have the time to deal with the problem in hand. If GPs had more time to talk about disease prevention to their patients when they first join the practice as children and to drive home to them the importance of healthy living, then it follows that they would have to spend less time fire-fighting later on.

The case for a children's public health strategy is certainly compelling. Not only do we stand on the brink of an obesity epidemic that could wipe years off children's lives, but poverty still condemns thousands of children every year to a lifetime of poor health followed by an early death.

A public health strategy aimed specifically at children would be a way of ensuring that this new momentum is not lost. With a National Service Framework for Children due to be published shortly by the Government, the timing would be perfect.

Moreover, even a relatively small sum of money could make a real difference. As this pamphlet shows, there are scores of high visibility, cost effective measures that can be quickly and easily introduced that will have a material effect on the health prospects of children.

It is therefore that rare thing in politics, something which both captures the public imagination, appeals to the Treasury and most importantly is able to deliver real and lasting benefits to one of the most vulnerable sections of the community. What Government could resist?

References

1. 'The Obesity Pandemic: will parents outlive their children?' Professor Andrew Prentice, Paper given at the British Association Science Festival, 2002

2. 'Fat kids equals fat profits: are we exploiting our children's health?', All-Party Parliamentary Group on Obesity Second Report, 2002

3. 'Tackling Obesity in England', House of Commons Committee of Public Accounts Ninth Report, 2002

4. 'NHS acute sector expenditure for Diabetes: the present, future and excess in-patient cost of care', CJ Currie et al, Diabetic Medicine 14, 1997

5. 'Why is Manchester so bad for your health?', The *Guardian*, 12 November 2002

6. 'Culinary Curriculum', Bee Wilson, New Statesman, 8 April 2002

7. 'Fat chance', The *Guardian*, 11 September 2002

8. 'Too thirsty for knowledge', BBC News Online, 8 October 2002

9. 'TV Dinners - What's being served up by the advertisers', Sustain, 2001

10. 'Parents show football snacks the red card', The Food Commission, 10 June 2002

11. Paper given by the Swedish Institute for public health at the European Society of Cardiology Annual Meeting, 2 September 2002

12. 'Obesity and the Food Industry: cause and effect?' All-Party Parliamentary Group on Obesity First Report, 2002

13. *Poverty Bites: Food, health and poor families*, E Dowler, Turner and B Dobson, Child Poverty Action Group, 2001

14. *Poverty and Social Exclusion in Britain*, The Joseph Rowntree Foundation, September 2000

15. *Poor Expectations: Poverty and undernourishment in pregnancy*, J Dallison and T Lobstein, Maternity Alliance and NCH Action for Children

16. *Retailing, sustainability and neighbourhood regeneration*, The Joseph Rowntree Foundation, 2001

17. Rural closures hit poor and elderly, BBC News Online, 6 October 1998

18. 'Fat Chance', The *Guardian*, 24 September 2002

19. 'Get Off the Couch', A MORI study commissioned by BUPA, 2001

20. 'Play Space', A survey by the Children's Society and the Children's Play Council, 2001

21. *Saving Lives, Saving Money. Physical Activity - the best buy in public health*, The Central Council of Physical Education, 2002

22. 'Bus Fares cut call for schools', BBC News Online, 13 January 2000

23. Department of Health Press Release, 20 November 2002